# cooking the Hungarian way

Paprika chicken is often eaten with small, buttery dumplings called *galuska*. (Recipes on pages 30 and 31.)

# cooking the
# Hungarian way

MAGDOLNA HARGITTAI

PHOTOGRAPHS BY ROBERT L. & DIANE WOLFE

easy menu
*ethnic*
cookbooks

**Lerner Publications Company ▪ Minneapolis**

Editor: Vicki Revsbech
Drawings by Jeanette Swofford
Map by Larry Kaushansky

The publisher wishes to thank Olga Zortai for her
assistance in the preparation of this book.

Photograph on page 8 courtesy of the Hungarian News and
Information Service. Photograph on page 12 by István Hargittai.

The page border for this book is based on the edge decoration
of a tablecloth from southern Hungary.

*To my American friends who kindly tasted my Hungarian
dishes and to Fay Leipheimer and Barbara Lowrey for
their friendship and cooperation*

Library of Congress Cataloging-in-Publication Data

Hargittai, Magdolna.
  Cooking the Hungarian way.

  (Easy menu ethnic cookbooks)
  Includes index.
  Summary: An introduction to the cooking of Hungary,
including recipes for such dishes as goulash, stuffed
peppers, and paprika chicken. Also discusses the
geography and history of this central European country.
  1. Cookery, Hungarian—Juvenile literature.
2. Hungary—Social life and customs—Juvenile literature.
[1. Cookery, Hungarian. 2. Hungary—Social life and
customs] I. Wolfe, Robert L., ill. II. Wolfe, Diane,
ill. III. Title. IV. Series.
TX723.5.H8H35  1986     641.59439     86-10661
ISBN 0-8225-0916-4 (lib. bdg.)

Manufactured in the United States of America

1  2  3  4  5  6  7  8  9  10  95  94  93  92  91  90  89  88  87  86

**Creamed spinach is served with fried rolls for a
simple, tasty meal. (Recipes on pages 40 and 41.)**

# CONTENTS

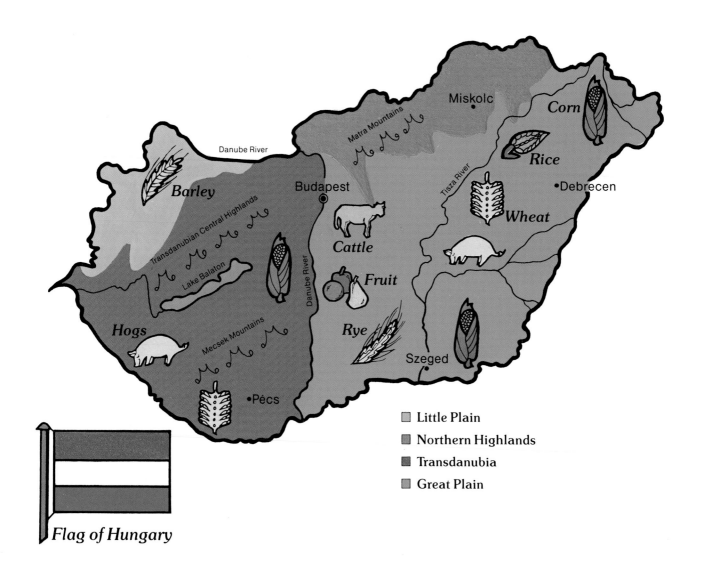

Miskolc

Corn

Matra Mountains

Danube River

Rice

Barley

Budapest

Debrecen

Transdanubian Central Highlands

Tisza River

Cattle

Wheat

Lake Balaton

Hogs

Fruit

Mecsek Mountains

Rye

Danube River

•Pécs

Szeged

☐ Little Plain

☐ Northern Highlands

☐ Transdanubia

☐ Great Plain

*Flag of Hungary*

# INTRODUCTION

What do you think of when you hear someone mention the country of Hungary? Gypsies in colorful costumes singing emotional love songs? Or composers like Franz Liszt and Béla Bartók, whose music embodies rhythmic folk tunes? Perhaps you remember reading about the Austro-Hungarian Empire, the country that played such an important role in European history during the 19th and early 20th centuries. Certainly you think of Hungarian goulash, that savory soup seasoned with generous amounts of the red spice paprika.

All these things are a part of the heritage of Hungary, a small central European country with a long and dramatic history. Throughout Hungary's 1,000 years of existence, its people have experienced many invasions by foreign powers and have lived under many kinds of government. In good times and in bad, music and food have been important elements in Hungarian life. Today the music of Hungary's composers and musicians can still be heard in concert halls all over the world, and delicious Hungarian dishes like goulash and strudel are enjoyed by people everywhere.

## THE LAND

Hungary is one of the few countries in Europe that is surrounded by land on all sides. It is bordered by Czechoslovakia to the north, the Soviet Union and Romania to the east, Yugoslavia to the south, and Austria to the west. About three-fourths of the country is farmland, and most of this land is divided into either state or collective farms. Hungary's most important crops are wheat and corn, and its warm, sunny summers create ideal conditions for a large harvest of fruits and vegetables.

Hungary is divided into four regions. The largest region, the *Great Plain*, lies east of the Danube River and south of the Matra Mountains. This lowland plain contains some of Europe's best farmland, and Hungary's longest river, the Tisza, flows through this region. *Transdanubia* lies across the Danube River from the Great Plain. This land of rolling hills and low mountains is home to Lake Balaton, central Europe's largest lake,

The majestic Danube River flows through the center of the city of Budapest.

also known as the Hungarian Sea. Hungary's two smallest regions are located in the north. To the northwest is the *Little Plain*, which is mostly flat farmland. The rugged, heavily forested *Northern Highlands* in the northeast is the country's most mountainous region.

The capital city of Budapest is often called "the Queen of the Danube" because it lies on the famous Danube River. The cities of Buda and Pest united to form Budapest in 1872. The part of the city that was once Buda lies on the Transdanubian side of the Danube and, like the rest of the region, is hilly. The area once called Pest is located on the Great Plain side of the river and is where most of the inhabitants of Budapest live.

## THE HISTORY

In the ninth century, a group of nomads called Magyars migrated from their home near the Ural Mountains to present-day Hungary. The Magyars settled in the grasslands along the Danube River where they found grazing land for their sheep and cattle. The Hungarian people trace their ancestry back to this group of nomads and still call themselves Magyars.

Hungary's first monarch, King Stephen I (997-1038 A.D.), was a strong leader who converted the Magyars to Christianity and united them under a central government. Much of the good done by King Stephen, however, was undone by the weak kings who followed him, making Hungary an easy target for the Mongols who invaded in the mid-13th century. Fortunately for the Hungarians, the Mongols left when their leader died.

The reign of King Matthias Corvinus (1458-1490) was a high point in Hungarian history. King Matthias not only had a strong government backed by a powerful army, but he also made Hungary an important cultural center by sponsoring artists and scholars. This period was also an outstanding time in Hungarian culinary history. Traditional Hungarian ways of cooking were blended with more formal western European techniques, and chefs were considered so important that they were elevated to the level of wealthy landowners.

In 1526, Hungary was the victim of another invasion when they were defeated by the Turks in the Battle of Mohács. The Turks took over most of the country, and their harsh rule lasted until the end of the 1600s when they were defeated by the Habsburgs of Austria. The Habsburgs ruled Hungary with a heavy hand until an uprising lasting from 1703 until 1711 forced them to treat the Hungarians with respect.

The mid-19th century was a time of revolution in many countries in Europe, and Hungary was no exception. The Habsburgs put down a Hungarian revolt in 1849. But by 1867, Austria had lost two wars, and Hungary was able to force the weakened country to form the Dual Monarchy of Austria-Hungary. This arrangement made Austria and Hungary two equal countries with one ruler. Although this gave Hungary more control over its own affairs, many Hungarians still wanted complete independence.

In 1914, the heir to the Austro-Hungarian throne was assassinated, which led to the beginning of World War I when Austria-Hungary declared war on Serbia. Shortly after Austria-Hungary's defeat at the end of the war, Hungary declared itself a republic.

In World War II, Hungary became an ally of Nazi Germany when Adolph Hitler promised to restore some of the territory that Hungary had lost in World War I. But Hitler soon turned on his Hungarian allies and controlled the country until the Germans were defeated in 1945. Hungary became a Communist country soon after the end of the war.

Today Hungary is an independent nation with a rather relaxed Communist government. One out of every five of Hungary's 10 million people live in the capital city. The national language is Hungarian or, as the natives call it, Magyar—a name that brings to mind the nomads who were the first Hungarians.

## THE FOOD

During their migration and in their wars, the Hungarians always gained some new knowledge to enrich their cuisine. The two groups that have had the most lasting impact on Hungarian cooking are the Magyars and the Turks.

The Magyars, the ancestors of the Hungarian people, were nomads who favored food that would travel well without spoiling. One common Magyar dish was *gulyás*, a soup made by drying cubes of meat that had been cooked with onions. This "instant" soup took up very little space and, when mixed with hot water, made a fast and filling meal. Today *gulyás*, or goulash, is still a favorite Hungarian dish. Although the recipe has changed over the years—it is no longer dried and can include anything from green peppers to tomatoes—it owes its beginnings to the Magyar's simple soup.

Another Hungarian specialty that dates back to the Magyars is *tarhonya*, a pasta made of a flour and egg dough that has been crumbled into pea-sized balls and dried. Because it could be stored indefinitely, this pasta was very convenient for the migrating life of the nomads.

The Magyars also introduced a cooking utensil called a *bogrács*. A *bogrács* is a copper or cast iron kettle that is suspended from a sturdy stick over an open fire. Hungarians still use a *bogrács* on cookouts when making a dish such as goulash or fish stew. In many restaurants, these dishes are served in a mini-*bogrács* over a flame.

If any one ingredient can be singled out as most characteristic of Hungarian cooking,

it has to be paprika, a spice made of ground dried red peppers. No one is quite sure where Hungarian paprika came from, but it first appeared in Hungary in the 16th century during the Turkish occupation. At first, paprika was used only by the lower classes, but it was eventually discovered by the nobility and became an essential part of Hungarian cuisine by the middle of the 19th century. In 1937, Hungarian professor Albert Szent-Gyorgyi won the Nobel Prize for physiology and medicine when he discovered that paprika is the world's richest source of vitamin C.

Paprika can be quite hot, and many people have come to associate Hungary with very spicy food. For a meal to be typically Hungarian, however, the paprika need not be terribly strong. Powdered paprika comes in a great variety of strengths, from mild and slightly sweet to red hot, so there is a paprika to please every taste.

Strudel and coffee are two Hungarian treats that were also introduced during the Turkish occupation. The Turks ate a delicious pastry made of paper-thin sheets of dough, called phyllo, that were baked with nuts and

Some ingredients commonly used in Hungarian cooking, such as potatoes, onions, and peppers, are displayed at this open-air market.

honey. The Hungarians took the phyllo dough and filled it with a variety of sweet fillings, such as cherries or poppy seeds, to make strudel. Coffee, a perfect accompaniment to strudel, was introduced to Hungary at the same time as phyllo dough. A small cup of very strong coffee with sugar and milk or cream, or even without, is an important part of a Hungarian meal.

Today the traditional, often heavy Hungarian meals have given way to lighter fare. But hospitality is a national pastime in Hungary, and even the most ardent weight-watchers give up their diets on holidays and during special get-togethers with friends and relatives. At the beginning of a meal, Hungarians wish a good appetite to each other by saying, *"Jó étvágyat kivánok"* (YO ATE-vah-dyat KEE-vah-nok). When they finish eating, they thank their host or hostess by saying *"Köszönöm"* (KOH-soh-nohm). The answer is also my wish to you: *"Váljék kedves egészségére"* (VAH-lyake KEHD-vesh EH-gase-shay-gay-reh), which means "let it be to your health!"

# BEFORE YOU BEGIN

Cooking any dish, plain or fancy, is easier and more fun if you are familiar with its ingredients. Hungarian cooking makes use of some ingredients that you may not know. You should also be familiar with the special terms that will be used in various recipes in this book. Therefore, *before* you start cooking any of the dishes in this book, study the following "dictionary" of special ingredients and terms very carefully. Then read through each recipe you want to try from beginning to end.

Now you are ready to shop for ingredients and to organize the cookware you will need. Once you have assembled everything, you can begin to cook. It is also very important to read *The Careful Cook* on page 44 before you start. Following these rules will make your cooking experience safe, fun, and easy.

## COOKING UTENSILS

*colander* — A bowl with holes in the bottom and sides. It is used for draining liquid from a solid food.

*cruet* — A slender, glass bottle with a tight-fitting top, used to prepare and store salad dressing

*Dutch oven* — A heavy pot with a tight-fitting domed lid that is often used for cooking soups or stews

*pastry brush* — A small brush with nylon bristles used for coating food with melted butter or other liquids

*sieve* — A bowl-shaped utensil made of wire mesh used to wash or drain small, fine foods

*spatula* — A flat, thin utensil, usually metal, used to lift, toss, turn, or scoop up food

## COOKING TERMS

*beat* — To stir rapidly in a circular direction

*boil* — To heat a liquid over high heat until bubbles form and rise rapidly to the surface

*brown* — To cook food quickly in fat over high heat so that the surface turns an even brown

*core* — To remove the center part of a fruit or vegetable that contains the stem and/or seed

*cream* — To beat several ingredients together until the mixture has a smooth consistency

*fold* — To blend an ingredient with other ingredients by using a gentle overturning circular motion instead of by stirring or beating

*garnish* — To decorate with a small piece of food such as parsley

*knead* — To work dough by pressing it with the palms, pushing it outward, and then pressing it over on itself

*pinch* — A very small amount, usually what you can pick up between your thumb and forefinger

*preheat* — To allow an oven to warm up to a certain temperature before putting food in it

*sauté* — To fry quickly over high heat in oil or fat, stirring or turning to prevent burning *seed* — To remove seeds from a food

*simmer* — To cook over low heat in liquid kept just below its boiling point. Bubbles may occasionally rise to the surface.

## SPECIAL INGREDIENTS

*bay leaf* — The dried leaf of the bay (also called laurel) tree. It is often used to season food.

*bread crumbs* — Tiny pieces of stale bread made by crushing the bread with the bottom of a glass or rolling pin. Packaged bread crumbs can be bought at grocery stores.

*caraway seeds* — Aromatic seeds used in cooking

*cinnamon* — A spice used ground or in sticks to flavor food

*cinnamon sugar* — A mixture of cinnamon and sugar. You can make your own by mixing one part cinnamon with three parts sugar.

*cloves* — An aromatic spice used whole or ground in cooking

*dry mustard* — A powder made from the dried seed of the mustard plant

*farina* — A cereal made of finely-ground grain

*paprika* — A powder made from the ground, dried pods of the *capsicum* pepper plant

*parsnip* — The long, white, sweet-tasting root vegetable of the parsnip plant

*peppercorns* — The berries of an East Indian plant. Peppercorns are used both whole and ground (pepper) to flavor food.

*phyllo* — Paper-thin dough, which can be wrapped around a sweet filling to make strudel. Phyllo is available frozen at many supermarkets and specialty stores.

*pinto beans* — Spotted beans that are about the size and shape of kidney beans

*poppy seed pastry filling* — A thick, sweet mixture made from poppy seeds and corn syrup that is used in making pies, cakes, and breads

*poppy seeds* — The seed of the poppy, often used in baking

*scallions* — A variety of green onion

# A HUNGARIAN MENU

Below is a menu for a typical day of Hungarian cooking. The Hungarian names of the dishes are given along with a guide on how to pronounce them. *Recipe included in book*

| ENGLISH | HUNGARIAN | PRONUNCIATION GUIDE |
|---|---|---|
| **Breakfast** | **Reggeli** | REH-geh-lee |
| I | I | |
| *Hungarian scrambled eggs | Tojásrántotta | TOH-yawsh-ran-tah-tah |
| Rolls and butter | Zsemlye és vaj | JEM-yeh AYSH VOY |
| Tea | Tea | TAY-ah |
| II | II | |
| *Hungarian cold plate | Hidegtál | HEE-deg-tahl |
| Rolls and butter | Zsemlye és vaj | JEM-yeh AYSH VOY |
| Milk and coffee | Tej és kávé | TAY AYSH KAH-vay |
| **Dinner** | **Ebéd** | EH-bayd |
| *Informal* | *Hétköznapi* | HATE-kuhz-no-pee |
| I | I | |
| *Goulash or dry bean soup with smoked sausage | Gulyásleves vagy bableves füstölt kolbásszal | GOO-yawsh-leh-vesh VUDGE BOB-leh-vesh FYOOSH-tult KOL-bah-sol |
| *Noodles with cottage cheese | Túrós csusza | TOO-rohsh CHOH-sah |
| Coffee | Kávé | KAH-vay |
| II | II | |
| *Stuffed green peppers in tomato sauce | Töltött paprika | TUL-tut PAP-ree-kah |

| ENGLISH | HUNGARIAN | PRONUNCIATION GUIDE |
|---|---|---|
| *Strudel | Rétes | RAY-tesh |
| Coffee | Kávé | KAH-vay |
| III | III | |
| *Paprika potatoes | Paprikás burgonya | PAP-ree-kash BOOR-goh-nyah |
| *Green pepper salad | Paprikasaláta | PAP-ree-kah-shoh-lah-tah |
| Tea | Tea | TAY-ah |
| *Formal* | *Ünnepi* | YOO-neh-pee |
| I | I | |
| *Cold cherry soup | Hideg meggyleves | HEE-dehg MEDG-leh-vesh |
| *Fried pork or veal with | Rántott szelet | RON-tut SEH-let |
| mashed potatoes | burgonyapürével | BOOR-goh-nyah-puh-reh-vehl |
| *Tomato salad | Paradicsomsaláta | POH-roh-dee-chom-shoh-lah-tah |
| *Strudel | Rétes | RAY-tesh |
| Coffee | Kávé | KAH-vay |
| II | II | |
| *Eggs "Casino" | Kaszinótojás | KOH-see-noo-toh-yawsh |
| *Újházi chicken soup | Újházi tyúkleves | OOY-hah-zee TYOOK-leh-vesh |
| *Paprika chicken with | Paprikás csirke | PAP-ree-kash CHIR-keh |
| dumplings | galuskával | GOH-lush-kah-vahl |
| *Cucumber salad | Uborkasaláta | OO-bor-kah-shoh-lah-tah |
| *Strudel | Rétes | RAY-tesh |
| Coffee | Kávé | KAH-vay |
| **Supper** | *Vacsora* | VOH-choh-rah |
| I | I | |
| *Újházi chicken soup | Újházi tyúkleves | OOY-hah-zee TYOOK-leh-vesh |
| Milk or tea | Tej vagy tea | TAY VUDGE TAY-ah |
| II | II | |
| *Creamed spinach with | Spenótfőzelék | SHPEH-note-foh-seh-lake |
| fried rolls | bundás kenyérrel | BOON-dawsh KEH-nyehr-el |
| Milk | Tej | TAY |

# BREAKFAST/
Reggeli

Some Hungarians like to eat a light breakfast of rolls with butter and jam or honey. Others, especially those who live in the country, prefer a more substantial morning meal of salami, ham, or sausage; cheese; eggs (prepared in any of a variety of ways); fresh green pepper rings; tomato slices; and rolls and butter. Any breakfast, however, is usually accompanied by tea or strong coffee for the adults and milk or cocoa for the children.

# Hungarian Cold Plate/
Hidegtál

*In Hungary, cold plate is eaten at almost any time of the day. It can be served at breakfast or supper or as an appetizer at a party or formal dinner.*

½ **pound smoked sausage, cut into ½-inch pieces**
½ **pound salami, sliced**

4 **to 6 slices ham**
2 **to 3 hard-cooked eggs, shelled and cut in half lengthwise**
2 **medium red peppers, seeded and cut into strips**
2 **medium green peppers, seeded and cut into strips**
4 **medium tomatoes, sliced**
1 **medium cucumber, peeled and sliced**
  **various cheeses**
  **pickles**
  **radishes**
  **scallions**

Arrange all ingredients on a large plate and serve with rolls and butter.

*Serves 4 to 6*

# Hungarian Scrambled Eggs/ Tojásrántotta

*Four strips of bacon cut into small pieces can be substituted for the smoked sausage.*

**8 eggs**
**½ teaspoon salt**
**¼ pound smoked sausage, cut into ½-inch pieces**
**1 medium onion, peeled and chopped**
**1 medium green pepper, seeded and cut into rings**
**½ teaspoon paprika**

1. In a medium bowl, beat eggs lightly. Stir in salt and set aside.
2. In a large frying pan, fry sausage over medium heat. Add onion and green pepper and sauté until onion is transparent.
3. Add egg mixture and cook, scrambling with a spoon, until eggs are set.
4. Sprinkle with paprika and serve hot.

*Serves 3 to 4*

**Scrambled eggs become a special dish when cooked with green pepper rings and smoked sausage.**

Hungarian cold plate *(front)* and eggs "Casino" *(back)* are two popular appetizers that can be prepared ahead of time and refrigerated until they are served. (Recipes on pages 18 and 21.)

# DINNER/
# Ebéd

The main meal in Hungary is usually eaten between noon and 2:00 P.M. Informal dinners consist of soup, a main dish with salad, and dessert. More elaborate formal dinners, which take place later in the day, start with an appetizer followed by soup, one or two main dishes with salad, and dessert.

# Eggs "Casino"
# Kaszinótojás

*This appetizer was introduced in Budapest in the 1920s and quickly became very popular.*

**4 hard-cooked eggs, shells removed**
**6 tablespoons sour cream**
**1½ teaspoons dry mustard**
**¾ teaspoon powdered sugar**
**¼ teaspoon salt**
**¼ cup plus 2 tablespoons mayonnaise**
**1 17-ounce can mixed vegetables, drained**

**½ teaspoon chopped parsley for garnish**

1. Cut ½ inch off the wide end of each egg. With a pointed knife, gently remove egg yolks without tearing whites.
2. In a medium bowl, mash yolks with a fork until smooth. Add 2 tablespoons sour cream, 1 teaspoon mustard, ¼ teaspoon powdered sugar, and salt and mix well. Fill eggs with yolk mixture.
3. In a medium bowl, make vegetable salad by combining ¼ cup mayonnaise, 2 tablespoons sour cream, ¼ teaspoon sugar, and a pinch of salt. Add vegetables to mayonnaise mixture and stir well.
4. In a medium bowl, make tartar sauce by mixing 2 tablespoons mayonnaise, 2 tablespoons sour cream, ½ teaspoon mustard, and ¼ teaspoon powdered sugar.
5. Arrange salad on 4 small plates or in small bowls. Put an egg with the open side down in the center of each plate. Pour tartar sauce over eggs and sprinkle with chopped parsley.

*Serves 4*

Hungarian soups can be cold and creamy like cold cherry soup *(left)* or steaming hot and hearty like dry bean soup with smoked sausage *(right).*

# Dry Bean Soup with Smoked Sausage/
## Bableves Füstölt Kolbásszal

*Pinched noodles called csipetke (see page 25) are often served with this soup for a delicious, filling meal. Any leftover soup can be refrigerated and eaten in the next few days—some people think it's even better that way!*

½ **pound dried pinto beans**
2 **tablespoons vegetable oil**
1 **small onion, peeled and chopped**
2 **tablespoons flour**
1½ **teaspoons paprika**
5 **cups water**
1 **or 2 bay leaves**
1 **teaspoon salt**
1 **medium carrot, peeled and cut into thin 3-inch-long slices**
1 **small parsnip, peeled and cut into thin 3-inch-long slices**
½ **pound smoked sausage**
1½ **teaspoons white vinegar**
½ **cup sour cream**

1. In a colander, rinse beans well under cold water and let drain. Place beans in a medium bowl, add enough water to cover, and let soak overnight.
2. Drain beans in a colander.
3. In a kettle or Dutch oven, heat oil over medium heat for 1 minute. Add onion and sauté until transparent. Add flour and cook, stirring constantly, until light brown.
4. Add beans, paprika, 5 cups water, bay leaves, salt, carrot, and parsnip to kettle and stir. Cover and simmer over low to medium-low heat for about 30 minutes.
5. Cut sausage into 1-inch pieces and add to soup. Cook for 30 minutes more or until beans are tender.
6. Just before serving, add vinegar and stir. Place 1 cup of hot soup in a small bowl, add sour cream, and stir until smooth. Add sour cream mixture to kettle and stir well. Serve hot.

*Serves 4*

# Cold Cherry Soup/
## Hideg Meggyleves

*This rather unusual soup is especially popular in the hot summer months.*

1 20- or 21-ounce can cherry pie
    filling, sweetened or unsweetened
1 can water
1 cinnamon stick
2 teaspoons cinnamon sugar
20 whole cloves
3 slices lemon peel
2 tablespoons lemon juice
2 tablespoons sugar (if pie filling is
    unsweetened)
1 pint light cream or half and half

1. In a large saucepan, mix pie filling and water. Add all remaining ingredients except cream and stir well.
2. Bring to a boil over medium-high heat. Boil for 1 minute, stirring constantly.
3. Cool to room temperature and add cream. Stir and refrigerate. Serve cold.

*Serves 6*

# Goulash/
## Gulyásleves

*Although many people think that goulash is a thick stew, the genuine Hungarian goulash is actually a substantial soup. It is often served as a main dish followed by a non-meat second dish or a dessert.*

1 pound beef hind rump or round roast
1 pound beef chuck
3 tablespoons vegetable oil
½ cup finely chopped onion
1 tablespoon paprika
1 teaspoon salt
1 teaspoon caraway seeds
2 tablespoons tomato paste
1 cup beef broth
4 medium potatoes
8 cups (2 quarts) water
1 medium green pepper, seeded
    and cut into strips

1. Cut meat into 1-inch cubes. (Meat is easier to cut if slightly frozen.)
2. In a kettle or Dutch oven, heat oil over

medium heat for 1 minute. Add onions and sauté until transparent.

3. Add paprika, beef cubes, salt, and caraway seeds and cook for about 10 minutes, stirring frequently.

4. In a small bowl, stir tomato paste into ½ cup beef broth. Add to beef mixture and stir. Simmer for 30 minutes.

5. Peel potatoes and cut into bite-size pieces.

6. Add potatoes, remaining beef broth, and 8 cups water to kettle. Bring to a boil and simmer for 15 minutes.

7. Return soup to a boil, add pepper strips and *csipetke*, and cook for 10 more minutes.

### *Csipetke:*

**½ cup flour**
**pinch of salt**
**1 egg**
**1 teaspoon water (optional)**

1. In a medium bowl, combine flour, salt, and egg.

2. Knead until flour is absorbed, forming a stiff dough. Add 1 teaspoon water if necessary.

3. Flatten the dough between your palms until it is about ⅛ inch thick. Pinch off ½-inch pieces of dough and drop into boiling soup.

*Serves 4 to 6*

An authentic Hungarian goulash includes at least two kinds of meat.

# Salad Dressing
## Saláta Öntet

*This is Hungary's most popular salad dressing. All of the following salads use some variation of this dressing, and any additional seasonings are mentioned in the salad recipes.*

½ **cup white vinegar**
1 **cup water**
2 **tablespoons salad oil**
1 **teaspoon salt**
1 **teaspoon sugar**

1. Pour all ingredients into a cruet or jar, close tightly, and shake well.
2. Pour over salad and refrigerate for 1 hour.

# Tomato Salad/
## Paradicsomsaláta

6 **to 8 firm medium tomatoes**
   **dressing**
1 **tablespoon finely chopped parsley**

1. Slice tomatoes with a sharp knife and place in a large bowl.
2. Pour dressing over tomatoes and refrigerate for 1 hour.
3. Sprinkle with parsley before serving.

*Serves 4*

# Green Pepper Salad/
## Paprikasaláta

1 **medium onion, peeled**
4 **to 6 medium green peppers**
   **dressing**
½ **teaspoon paprika**

1. Slice onion thinly and separate the rings. Core peppers and cut into thin rings. Place in a medium bowl.
2. Pour dressing over onions and peppers and mix well. Refrigerate for 1 hour.
3. Sprinkle with paprika before serving.

*Serves 4*

Hungarian salads such as green pepper salad *(left)*, cucumber salad *(center)*, and tomato salad *(right)* with vinegar and oil dressing are simple yet delicious additions to any meal.

# Cucumber Salad/
## Uborkasaláta

**2 medium cucumbers, peeled**
**1 teaspoon salt**
**1 clove garlic, peeled and crushed**
**2 tablespoons sour cream**
   **dressing (see page 27)**
**½ teaspoon paprika**
**¼ teaspoon pepper**

1. Cut cucumbers into thin slices and place in medium bowl. Add salt, mix well, and set aside for 30 minutes.
2. Add garlic and sour cream to dressing, cover tightly, and shake well.
3. Drain cucumbers in a colander and press out remaining liquid with hands.
4. Return cucumbers to bowl, add dressing, and mix well. Refrigerate for 1 hour.
5. Sprinkle with paprika and pepper before serving.

*Serves 4*

# Paprika Potatoes/
## Paprikás Burgonya

*Paprika potatoes can also be made with frankfurters.*

**6 to 8 medium potatoes**
**2 tablespoons vegetable oil**
**1 medium onion, peeled and chopped**
**1 teaspoon paprika**
**1 teaspoon salt**
**½ pound smoked sausage**

1. Peel and quarter potatoes, place in large pan, and cover with cold water.
2. Add oil to kettle and sauté onion over medium heat until transparent.
3. Drain potatoes in a colander. Add potatoes, paprika, and salt to kettle. Add enough water to cover potatoes and mix well. Simmer over medium-low heat for 20 minutes or until potatoes are tender.
4. Cut meat into ½-inch pieces and add to potatoes. Simmer 5 more minutes and serve hot.

*Serves 4*

# Paprika Chicken/ Paprikás Csirke

*Serve paprika chicken with* galuska *(see page 31) or with noodles prepared according to package directions.*

1   2½- to 3-pound chicken, cut into
    8 pieces
4   tablespoons vegetable oil
1   large onion, peeled and
    finely chopped
1   teaspoon salt
1   tablespoon paprika
¾   cup water
1½  cups sour cream
1   tablespoon flour
1   green pepper, cored and cut
    into rings

1. Wash chicken pieces under cool running water and pat dry with paper towel.
2. In a kettle or Dutch oven, heat oil over medium heat for 1 minute. Add onion and sauté until transparent.
3. Place chicken pieces in Dutch oven and cook, turning often, until lightly browned on all sides.
4. Sprinkle salt and paprika on chicken and add ½ cup water. Cover and bring to a boil.
5. Reduce heat and simmer for about 30 minutes or until chicken is tender. Add more water if necessary, but only a small amount at a time. (Adding too much water will change the flavor of the chicken.)
6. In a small bowl, combine 1 cup sour cream, flour, and ¼ cup water and stir well. Pour mixture over chicken and stir. Simmer, uncovered, for 5 more minutes.
7. Place chicken in a deep serving dish. Cover with sour cream mixture and top with remaining sour cream. Garnish with green pepper rings.

*Serves 4*

# Small Dumplings/ Galuska

*Noodles and dumplings are popular additions to the good, hearty Hungarian soups and stews.* Galuska *can also be served with main dishes such as paprika chicken.*

**2 tablespoons butter or margarine**
**1 egg**
**1 cup milk**
**2 teaspoons salt**
**2 cups all-purpose flour**
**12 cups (3 quarts) water**

1. In a medium bowl, cream 1 tablespoon butter and stir in egg, milk, and 1 teaspoon salt.
2. Add flour, a little at a time, stirring well after each addition, until mixture is the consistency of cookie dough. If dough is too stiff, add 1 to 2 tablespoons milk or water.
3. In a kettle, bring water and 1 teaspoon salt to a boil over medium-high heat.
4. Dip a teaspoon in hot water, scoop up small pieces of dough (about ¼ teaspoon each), and drop carefully into boiling water. Dip spoon in hot water again if dough starts to stick.
5. Boil dumplings 2 to 3 minutes or until they rise to the surface. Drain in a colander.
6. Melt 1 tablespoon butter in a medium saucepan. Add dumplings and stir gently until well coated. Serve immediately.

*Serves 4*

Stuffed green peppers with tomato sauce and paprika potatoes are two dishes with a definite Hungarian flavor. (Recipes on pages 29 and 33.)

## Stuffed Green Peppers in Tomato Sauce/ Töltött Paprika

*This dish is especially popular in the summer and autumn when freshly-picked peppers are available.*

**6 large green peppers**
**1 cup rice (not instant)**
**1 cup water**
**2 tablespoons oil**
**¼ cup chopped onion**
**2 pounds ground pork or beef**
**2 eggs**
**2 teaspoons salt**
**½ teaspoon pepper**
**½ teaspoon paprika**

**Sauce:**

**1 29-ounce can tomato sauce**
**1 can water**
**roux (see page 40)**
**2 tablespoons sugar**

1. Wash green peppers, cut off and discard tops, and remove seeds.
2. In a medium pan, combine rice with 1 cup water, cover, and simmer over medium heat about 10 minutes or until water is absorbed.
3. In a small frying pan, heat oil for 1 minute over medium heat. Add onions and sauté until transparent.
4. In a large bowl, combine rice, onions, meat, eggs, salt, pepper, and paprika and mix thoroughly.
5. Fill the hollowed-out peppers with stuffing. (If there is stuffing left over, make large meatballs and cook them with the stuffed peppers.)
6. In a kettle or Dutch oven, combine tomato sauce with 1 can water. Stand peppers upright in tomato mixture and cook over medium-low heat for 30 minutes.
7. Prepare roux in a separate pan (see page 40). Add about ¼ cup of tomato mixture to roux and mix well. Pour roux into kettle with peppers, stir in sugar, and cook for another 10 minutes.

*Serves 6*

*Rántott szelet* is moist, flavorful pork or veal with a crispy crust.

# Fried Breaded Pork or Veal/ Rántott Szelet

*This typical central European dish originated in Vienna, where it is called* Wiener schnitzel.

**8 slices (about 2 pounds) thin pork chops or veal cutlets**
**1 teaspoon salt**
**2 eggs**
**½ cup flour**
**¾ cup bread crumbs**
**1½ cups vegetable oil**
**8 lemon slices for garnish**

1. Place each piece of meat between 2 pieces of wax paper and pound with a hammer or mallet until meat is about ¼ inch thick. (If using pork chops, first cut off and discard bones and excess fat.)
2. Salt both sides of each piece of meat and refrigerate for 30 minutes.
3. In a shallow dish, beat eggs slightly. Pour flour into another shallow dish and

bread crumbs into a third shallow dish.
4. Dip a slice of meat lightly in the flour.
Then dip it in the eggs, coating thoroughly,
and finally in the bread crumbs. Press bread
crumbs on meat slices with your hands.
The slices should be completely covered
with batter on both sides.
5. In a large frying pan, heat oil over
medium-high heat until hot enough to
brown a 1-inch cube of bread in 1 minute.
6. Fry meat 3 to 4 minutes per side or
until brown and crisp. Use a spatula to
turn them, being careful not to break the
crust and let the juices escape. Remove
from pan and drain on paper towels.
7. Place on a serving plate and garnish
with lemon slices. Serve hot.

*Serves 4*

# Noodles with Cottage Cheese/ Túrós Csusza

*To make this dessert a sweet dish,*
*omit bacon, mix drained noodles in*

*1 tablespoon butter instead of bacon fat,*
*and sprinkle with 2 tablespoons*
*powdered sugar.*

**1 8- to 10-ounce package wide egg**
   **noodles**
**2 to 3 slices bacon, cut into small**
   **pieces**
**1 cup small curd cottage cheese**
**1 cup sour cream**

1. Cook noodles according to directions
on package.
2. In a large saucepan, fry bacon until
nearly crisp. Drain on paper towel.
3. Drain noodles in a colander and add
to bacon fat. Stir well and cover.
4. In a medium saucepan, heat cottage
cheese and sour cream over medium
heat, stirring constantly, until hot.
5. Add half of cottage cheese mixture
to noodles and stir well. Place on a warm
serving dish, cover with remaining cottage
cheese mixture, and garnish with fried
bacon pieces.

*Serves 4*

For dessert, diners in Hungary enjoy both sweet, flaky strudel *(front)* and noodles with cottage cheese *(back)* flavored with the smoky taste of bacon.

# Strudel/
## Rétes

*Be sure to read* Working with Phyllo Dough *on page 39 before preparing strudels.*

**6 phyllo sheets (3 per roll)**
**6 tablespoons unsalted butter, melted**
**6 tablespoons powdered sugar, plus**
    **extra for sprinkling**
**1 recipe filling (pages 38 and 39)**

1. Preheat oven to 350°. Butter a 9- by 13-inch pan. Place a slightly damp, clean kitchen towel (not terry cloth) on a clean working surface.
2. Place 1 phyllo sheet on the towel. With a pastry brush, brush with melted butter and sprinkle with powdered sugar. Repeat with 2 more sheets.
3. Place half of the filling on the bottom third of the top sheet, leaving about 1 inch on each side (see diagram).
4. Fold in the 2 sides and, starting at the bottom, carefully roll up the sheets. If the dough begins to stick, hold the bottom corners of the towel with both hands and lift to loosen the dough.
5. Place roll seam side down in a buttered pan and brush with melted butter. Make a second roll with remaining filling. Bake for 30 minutes or until golden brown.
6. When strudel is cool enough to handle, cut into 1-inch slices, place on dessert plates, and sprinkle with powdered sugar.

*Makes 2 rolls (about 24 pieces)*

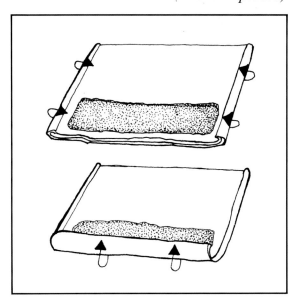

# Cottage Cheese Filling/ Túrós

 ¼ cup raisins
 ½ cup warm water
 1 egg, separated
 4 tablespoons sugar
16 ounces small curd cottage cheese
 8 ounces cream cheese, softened
 1 teaspoon grated lemon peel
 4 tablespoons farina cereal

1. In a small bowl, soak raisins in water for 10 minutes. Drain well in a colander.
2. Mix egg yolk with sugar until smooth and lemon colored. Add cottage cheese, cream cheese, raisins, lemon peel, and 2 tablespoons farina and mix well.
3. In a small bowl, beat egg white with a mixer or fork until it forms peaks. Fold into cottage cheese mixture.
4. Prepare strudels according to directions on page 37. Before spreading filling on dough, sprinkle bottom third of sheets with 1 tablespoon farina.

*Enough for 2 rolls*

# Poppy Seed Filling/ Mákos

6 ounces poppy seeds or 1 12½-ounce can Solo® poppy seed pastry filling
1 cup sugar
1 tablespoon sour cream
1 tablespoon strawberry jam
2 teaspoons grated lemon peel

1. In a medium bowl, mix poppy seeds and sugar. Grind mixture, about ½ cup at a time, in a coffee grinder or blender. (If using canned filling, omit sugar and do not grind.)
2. Return poppy seed mixture to bowl, add remaining ingredients, and mix well.
3. Prepare strudels according to directions on page 37.

*Enough for 2 rolls*

# Cherry Filling/ Meggyes

**2 16-ounce cans unsweetened tart cherries**
**6 tablespoons sugar**
**2 teaspoons cinnamon sugar (see page 15)**
**¼ cup almonds, finely chopped**
**2 tablespoons fine bread crumbs**

1. Drain cherries very thoroughly in a colander.
2. Prepare phyllo sheets according to steps 1 and 2 of the directions on page 37.
3. Instead of following step 3, do the following. Sprinkle the bottom third of the dough with 1 tablespoon bread crumbs. Spread half of cherries over bread crumbs, and top with 3 tablespoons sugar, 1 teaspoon cinnamon sugar, and 2 tablespoons almonds.
4. Follow steps 4 through 6 on page 37 to finish strudels.

*Enough for 2 rolls*

## WORKING WITH PHYLLO

Phyllo (FEE-low) dough is paper-thin dough made of flour and water that is available frozen in many supermarkets and in specialty stores. Phyllo is extremely fragile, but using it is not difficult if you follow these basic rules.

1. Thaw frozen phyllo in its original package for 24 hours in the refrigerator.
2. Do not unwrap phyllo until you are ready to use it. Make sure your work area is cleared, your melted butter and pastry brush are ready, and your filling is prepared.
3. Remove rings from your fingers and make sure your fingernails are not too long.
4. Work with one sheet at a time. Peel sheets carefully from package and cover remaining sheets tightly with either plastic wrap or a slightly damp kitchen towel (not terry cloth).
5. Leftover phyllo will stay fresh in the refrigerator for one week if wrapped in plastic wrap.
6. If phyllo is not available where you live, you can substitute frozen puff pastry, thawed and rolled very thin with a rolling pin. It won't be as thin as phyllo, though, so use one fewer layer than called for in the recipe.

# SUPPER/
# Vacsora

Because the main meal in Hungary is eaten in the middle of the day, the evening meal is usually lighter. It takes place between 5:30 and 8:00 P.M. when the family is home from work and school. Supper is usually a one course meal. It can be a soup, a vegetable dish, or very often a cold plate consisting of a wide variety of meats, cheeses, and vegetables.

# Roux/
# Rántás

*In Hungarian cooking, vegetables are nearly always prepared in a seasoned sauce that has been thickened with roux. The difference between American and Hungarian vegetable dishes has been compared to the difference between boiled meat and meat stew. Although the basic recipe for roux is always the same, additional seasonings are sometimes added.*

**1 tablespoon vegetable oil**
**3 tablespoons flour**
**⅓ cup water**

1. In a small saucepan, heat oil over low heat until warm (not hot).
2. Add flour and stir constantly until light brown. (Be careful not to burn.)
3. Remove from heat and stir in seasoning indicated in recipe.
4. Add ⅓ cup water and stir until smooth.

# Creamed Spinach
# with Fried Rolls/
# Spenótfőzelék
# Bundás Kenyérrel

*In Europe, spinach was probably first eaten in monasteries. Today, this nutritious vegetable is universally popular.*

**1¼ pounds (20 ounces) fresh spinach or 1 10-ounce package frozen chopped spinach, thawed**
**½ white bread roll**

**2 cups milk**
**1 teaspoon salt**
  **roux (see page 40)**
**1 clove garlic, peeled and crushed**

1. If using fresh spinach, discard tough stems and wash each leaf thoroughly.
2. In small bowl, soak roll in ½ cup milk.
3. In a large kettle or Dutch oven, bring 3 quarts water to a boil. Add spinach and return to a boil. Cook for 1 minute or until tender.
4. Drain spinach in a colander and press out remaining water with the back of a large spoon.
5. Put spinach, soaked roll, 1½ cups milk, and salt in a blender and blend on medium speed for about 30 seconds or until smooth. (If you don't have a blender, chop spinach well before mixing with remaining ingredients.) Pour into a large saucepan.
6. Prepare a roux with crushed garlic and add to spinach. Bring to a boil over medium heat, stirring constantly. Reduce heat and simmer for 5 to 10 minutes.

**Fried Rolls:**

**2 to 3 bread rolls**
**2 eggs**
**½ cup milk**
**¼ cup vegetable oil**

1. Cut rolls into ½-inch slices.
2. Beat eggs slightly in a shallow bowl, and pour milk into another shallow bowl.
3. In a medium frying pan, heat oil over medium heat for 1 minute.
4. Dip both sides of roll slices in milk (do not soak) and in eggs and carefully place in pan. Fry each side 3 to 5 minutes or until it begins to turn brown. Serve immediately.

*Serves 3 to 4*

Újházi chicken soup contains everything from parsnips to brussels sprouts and is filling enough to be served alone or with bread for supper.

# Újházi Chicken Soup/ Újházi Tyúkleves

*Újházi chicken soup was named after the famous 19th-century Hungarian actor Ede Újházi who liked to entertain his friends with this rich soup.*

 1 **3-pound chicken, cut into 8 pieces**
 2 **large carrots, peeled and cut**
    **into quarters**
 2 **medium parsnips, peeled and cut**
    **into quarters**
 ½ **pound brussels sprouts**
 1 **medium green pepper, seeded**
    **and cut in half**
 1 **stalk celery, cut in half**
1½ **cups (¼ pound) fresh sliced**
    **mushrooms**
 1 **medium onion, peeled**
 1 **to 2 cloves garlic, peeled**
 2 **teaspoons salt**
10 **peppercorns**
 ½ **teaspoon caraway seeds**
 1 **tablespoon tomato paste**
 ½ **teaspoon paprika**
 8 **cups (2 quarts) water**

 1 **cup canned sweet peas, drained**
 1 **cup very thin egg noodles**
 1 **tablespoon chopped parsley**
    **for garnish**

1. Wash chicken in cold water and place in large kettle or Dutch oven. Add all remaining ingredients except peas, noodles, and parsley.
2. Simmer over medium-low heat about 1 hour or until meat is tender, removing foam that forms on the surface of soup with a large spoon.
3. Carefully pour soup through a sieve with another large pan underneath to catch broth (do not discard). Set chicken and vegetables aside to cool.
4. When cool, remove chicken from bones and discard skin. Cut chicken and vegetables into bite-size pieces.
5. Reheat broth over medium heat. Add noodles and cook about 5 minutes until tender. Add meat, peas, and cooked vegetables and simmer for another 5 minutes. Sprinkle with chopped parsley before serving.

*Serves 6*

# THE CAREFUL COOK

Whenever you cook, there are certain safety rules you must always keep in mind.

1. Always wash your hands before handling food.
2. Thoroughly wash all raw vegetables and fruits to remove dirt and chemicals.
3. Use a cutting board when cutting up vegetables and fruits. Don't cut them up in your hand! And be sure to cut in a direction *away* from you and your fingers.
4. Long hair or loose clothing can catch fire if brought near the burners of a stove. If you have long hair, tie it back before cooking.
5. Turn all pot handles toward the back of the stove so that you will not catch your sleeves or jewelry on them. This is especially important when younger brothers and sisters are around. They could easily knock off a pot and get burned.
6. Always use a pot holder to steady hot pots or to take pans out of the oven. Don't use a wet cloth on a hot pan because the steam it produces could burn you.

7. Lift the lid of a steaming pot with the opening away from you so that you will not get burned.
8. If you get burned, hold the burn under cold running water. Do not put grease or butter on it. Cold water helps to take the heat out, but grease or butter will only keep it in.
9. If grease or cooking oil catches fire, throw baking soda or salt at the bottom of the flame to put it out. (Water will *not* put out a grease fire.) Call for help, and try to turn all the stove burners to "off."

# METRIC CONVERSION CHART

| WHEN YOU KNOW | | MULTIPLY BY | TO FIND | |
|---|---|---|---|---|
| **MASS (weight)** | | | | |
| ounces | (oz) | 28.0 | grams | (g) |
| pounds | (lb) | 0.45 | kilograms | (kg) |
| **VOLUME** | | | | |
| teaspoons | (tsp) | 5.0 | milliliters | (ml) |
| tablespoons | ((Tbsp) | 15.0 | milliliters | |
| fluid ounces | (oz) | 30.0 | milliliters | |
| cup | (c) | 0.24 | liters | (l) |
| pint | (pt) | 0.47 | liters | |
| quart | (qt) | 0.95 | liters | |
| gallon | (gal) | 3.8 | liters | |
| **TEMPERATURE** | | | | |
| Fahrenheit | (°F) temperature | 5/9 (after subtracting 32) | Celsius temperature | (°C) |

# COMMON MEASURES AND THEIR EQUIVALENTS

3 teaspoons = 1 tablespoon

8 tablespoons = ½ cup

2 cups = 1 pint

2 pints = 1 quart

4 quarts = 1 gallon

16 ounces = 1 pound

# INDEX
*(recipes indicated by* **bold face** *type)*

# ABOUT
# THE AUTHOR

**Magdolna Hargittai** (Magdi) was born and raised in Pécs, Hungary. She earned a doctorate in chemistry from Eötvös University and is a senior scientist at the Hungarian Academy of Sciences in Budapest. Magdi has always loved to cook and in her travels has had opportunities to become acquainted with the cuisines of Russia, Norway, Germany, and Italy. The Hargittais lived in the United States for two years while Magdi's husband, István, was a visiting professor at the University of Connecticut. During that time, Magdi enjoyed preparing genuine Hungarian meals for her American friends.

# easy menu *ethnic* cookbooks